D0547897

contents

Pages 4-5
What Are Living Things?

Pages 6-7
What Is a Bird?

Pages 8-9
Where Do They Live?

Pages 10-11
Bird Homes

Pages 12-13
What Do They Eat?

Pages 14-15
How Do They Breathe?

Pages 16-17
How Do They Move?

Pages 18-19
How Do They Grow?

Pages 20-21
Brilliant Birds

Pages 22-23
World Record Breakers

Page 24
Glossary & Index

THE
BOOK
COMPANY

©2019
**The Secret Book
Company**
King's Lynn
Norfolk PE30 4LS

ISBN: 978-1-912171-78-1

All rights reserved
Printed in Malaysia

Written by:
Grace Jones

Designed by:
Ian McMullen

A catalogue record for this book
is available from the British Library

What Are Living Things?

All living things move and grow.
Living things need air, food,
water and sunlight to
stay alive.

**These
are all
living
things.**

Frog

Tiger

Human

4

Knife, Fork and Plate

Books

These are all non-living things.

Teddy Bear

Non-living things do not move or grow. Non-living things do not need air, food, water or sunlight because they are not alive.

5

What Is a Bird?

Birds are living things that can live on land and on water. They need air, food, water and sunlight to live. Ostriches, penguins and owls are all types of bird.

Fact: There are over 10,000 known species of birds.

Ostrich

Penguin

Owl

Birds have two wings, can usually fly and have a backbone. They are warm-blooded animals. This means that their body temperature does not change when the temperature does.

A Snowy owl stays warm even when it is freezing cold because it is warm-blooded.

Where Do They Live?

This brightly coloured Toucan lives in the rainforests of South America.

All living things live in a **habitat** or home. Birds can live in many different habitats around the world. Some birds live in rainforests or woodland.

Other birds live in the many deserts and mountains that are found throughout the world.

This Mountain Bluebird lives in the mountains of North America.

Bird Homes

A bird's nest.

Most birds live in specially built homes, called nests. They are usually made out of mud, twigs, leaves and feathers. They build their nests in trees, on the ground or in rocky ledges. Nests provide them with shelter from **predators** and a home to raise their babies in.

10

Other birds migrate. This means that they do not stay in one home, but fly to different ones throughout the year. When the weather becomes colder, some birds will migrate to hotter **climates** to stay warm.

Fact:
Swallows migrate 10,000 miles from Europe to Africa every winter.

What Do They Eat?

Adult birds eat meat or plants and seeds, or a mixture of both. Some birds that eat other animals are called birds of prey. They have very good eyesight to find their food and strong feet to catch and hold onto their prey with.

A Golden Eagle.

Strong Feet

Other birds are omnivorous. This means that they eat both animals and plants. Emus are omnivorous birds; they eat fruit, seeds, plants and insects.

Emu

How Do They Breathe?

All birds breathe in oxygen from the air through their two lungs and extra air pouches. Unlike humans, birds' lungs do not change size when they breathe in or out.

Lungs

Birds breathe in and out through nostrils found at the top of their beaks. Their nostrils are called nares.

Nares

How Do They Move?

Wings

Tail

Muscles

Feathers

Most birds can fly through the air using their feathered wings. They use breast muscles to move their wings and the wind to help them fly high into the sky. They use their tails to change direction.

A Waved Albatross in flight.

16

Small, short
wings.

Penguin

Other birds, like penguins and ostriches, cannot fly
even though they have wings. Instead of flying, penguins
have learnt to swim to catch their food. Their small, short
wings helps them to travel through the water quicker.

How Do They Grow?

Most birds start life as babies inside their mother's eggs before they **hatch**. Some birds, like the Laysan Albatross lay just one egg at a time, whilst a female chicken can sit on several eggs at once.

Once they hatch, the baby birds have to stay in the nest because they cannot fly yet. When their wings have grown bigger and they are strong enough, thcy fly away from the nest.

Fact: Baby pigeons take around thirty days to leave the nest.

Brilliant Birds

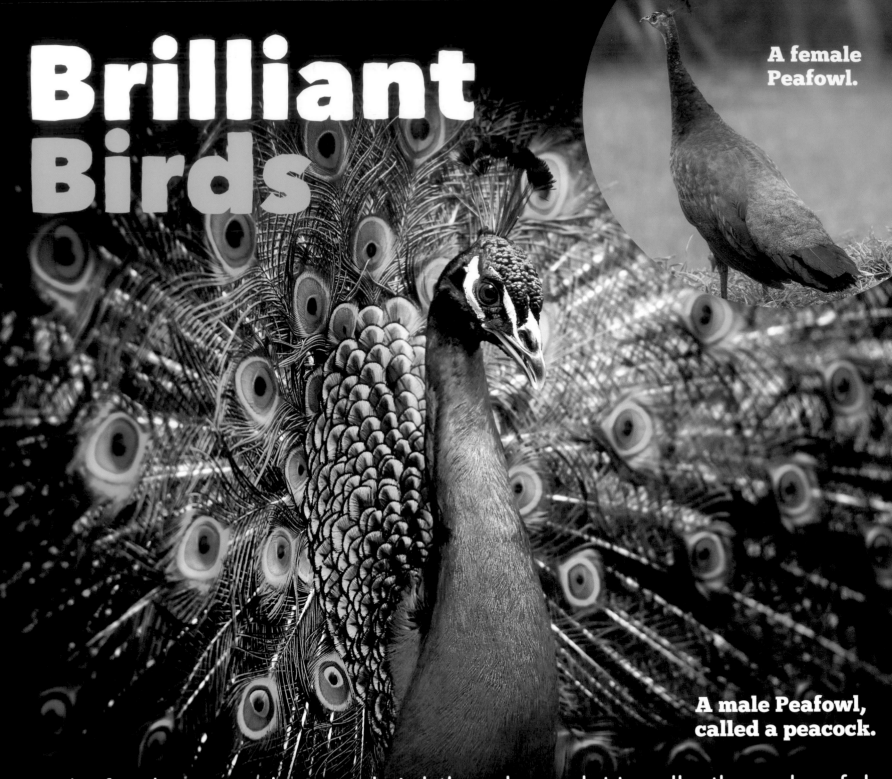

A female Peafowl.

A male Peafowl, called a peacock.

Birds' feathers can be very brightly coloured. Usually, the colourful birds we see are males. This is because the more colourful they are, the more likely it is female birds will choose them as their **mate**.

Some birds, like homing pigeons, are particularly smart. They have been used for thousands of years to carry messages from country to country. However far they have to travel, they can always find their way home again.

World Record Breakers

OSTRICH

Fact:
The ostrich is the **largest living bird**. It also lays the **largest eggs** and can run as fast as **60 miles per hour**.

Size:
Up to 2.7 metres tall

Record:
The World's Biggest Bird

BEE HUMMINGBIRD

Record: The World's Smallest Bird

Size: Up to 5 cm long

Fact: The smallest bird in the world weighs less than a few grains of rice!

Glossary

climates types of weather in particular places

habitat a home where animals and plants live

hatch when a baby animal or insect comes out of its egg

mate a partner who they choose to have their young with

predators any animal that eats other animals and insects

prey any animal or insect that is eaten by another

Index